Get Off Your Lazy Ass and Start Selling on eBay

Copyright © 2016 by Nick Vulich

Want to know about Nick's new book releases? Join our mailing list.

Interested in being notified when Nick releases his next book? Click here to join our mailing list. We promise not to send any spam, or unwanted emails, the only thing you will receive is news about Nick's new book releases.

Table of Contents

Getting Started 1

Why listen to me? 3

Why eBay 5

Dealing with Cassini Search and Best Match 7

Product Sourcing 10

Be a Seller First 14

Getting started 15

What Should You Sell? 18

eBay Selling 101 22

Let's Start Selling 25

Different Ways to Sell 27

Your First Listing 30

Write a Compelling Title 31

Picture it Sold 35

Craft a Great Description 38

Price Your Items to Sell 40

Ship Like a Pro 44

Customer Service Is Everything 48

My Story 51

Thank you 57

Bonus Excerpt 58
About the Author 69
Books by Nick Vulich 71

Getting Started

Right now, you're wanting to make more money. You're wanting to find a way to change your life. But you're not sure how, and it's driving you crazy.

Maybe you're looking for just a few extra bucks to help cover your expenses. Maybe you need a new car, and the money is not there. Or maybe it's more dramatic. Did you lose your job? Are you about ready to get the boot at work? Do you need to find a way to replace that lost income as quickly as possible?

You've tried everything—working overtime, help wanted ads, odd jobs around town. But, no matter what you try, it's not working. You're mad, and you're thinking nothing's working.

What do I do now?

It's frustrating, isn't it? If you're like me, you've probably read about all these other guys who made it big selling online, and thought what a bunch of BS. Nobody makes that kind of money selling online.

Does any of this sound familiar?

Here's what I want you to do. Forgot all of those negative thoughts for a few minutes. Instead, think about what you want to achieve. I know. It's hard. All the bad news, and bill collectors keep burning up your phone line, and assaulting your mailbox.

Forget all that stuff.

I want you to take five minutes, and think about you being successful. Imagine how it'd feel not to have any bills, or to be driving a new car, or just having some extra money to go out with the guys (or girls) every week.

It'd feel good, wouldn't it?

Trust me. You can have all that, and more if you're willing to work hard, and follow my directions.

Remember, I'm not promising you everything is going to be wine and roses. It's going to take time, effort, and a determination to succeed.

If you're willing to work at it, you can make as much money as you want selling online.

Before I tell you more about how to make money selling on eBay, let me tell you why I'm the guy you should listen to.

Why listen to me?

Hey there, Nick Vulich here.

If you're like me, I'm sure you're probably a little skeptical about taking advice from someone without knowing a little bit about them first.

I've been selling on eBay since 1999. Most of my online customers know me as history-bytes. I've also operated as its old news, back door video, and sports card one.

I've sold 30,004 items for a total of $411,755.44 over the past fifteen years, and that's just on my history-bytes id. I've cut way back on eBay selling over the past few years so I can focus on my writing, but I still keep my hat in the game. That way I can keep current with the challenges my readers face every day when they go to sell on eBay.

I've been an eBay Power Seller or Top Rated Seller for most of the past fifteen years, which means I've met eBay's sales and customer satisfaction goals.

This is a revised version of my first book, *Freaking Idiots Guide to Selling on eBay*. *Freaking Idiots Guide to Selling on eBay*, and *eBay Unleashed*, are aimed more towards how to get started selling on eBay. *eBay Subject Matter Expert* suggests a different approach to selling on eBay – building a platform where customers recognize you as an expert in your niche, and buy from you because of your knowledge in that field. *Sell It Online* gives a brief overview of selling on eBay, Amazon, Etsy, and Fiver. *How to Make Money Selling Old Books & Magazines on eBay* talks specifically about what I know best, how to sell books and magazines on eBay. *eBay Bookkeeping Made Easy* helps sellers understand how to keep track of the money they are making, and how to take advantage of the tax code to make even more money. *eBay Shipping Simplified* helps sellers determine the best way to ship their items, and how to use eBay's shipping tools to make the task easier. It also has a primer on international shipping, and using third party shipping providers such as Stamps.com and Endicia.

eBay 2015 covers everything sellers need to know to start and grow their eBay business. It takes an in depth look at several different ways to increase your eBay sales—Social Media Marketing, Email Marketing, and crowdfunding your business the use of strategically planned Kickstarter campaigns.

Taken as a whole, my books give you everything you need to be successful selling on eBay.

Why eBay

There are dozens of websites out there you can list and sell products on, but if you want to make money—eBay and Amazon are your best bets.

Here's why.

Each of these sites lets you tap into their existing customer base so you can begin making sales immediately. Each of these sites level the playing field by putting you on an equal footing with the big box stores.

When potential customers are looking at your listings online they don't know you're Joe Blow, selling from your recliner or kitchen table, unless you get careless, and post poor quality listings, littered with spelling errors, and grainy images.

Your success is entirely up to you, and how well you present the items you sell.

The big three websites for selling online are eBay, Amazon, and Etsy. eBay is best for listing collectibles, one of a kind, and used items. Amazon is best for selling new items, and used media products such as books, textbooks, DVDs, and computer software. Etsy is the go to place for selling crafts and handmade items.

Keep in mind, these are general rules. Most items will sell on all three sites, but if you want to maximize your profit potential you need to pick the site that's going to give you the biggest bang for your buck.

If I was a new seller just starting out, I'd post my first listings on eBay. The site is easy to use, draws tens of millions of visitors every day, and is a proven winner for small sellers After six months, or a year, when you've got things rolling, you can expand out to Amazon or Etsy.

Dealing with Cassini Search and Best Match

Cassini search is another factor that can cause problems for eBay sellers.

Many sellers have discovered Cassini Search / Best Match doesn't play well with listings that have HTML code in them, especially when it is at the top of the listing. A lot of sellers have noted their listings either doesn't come up in search at all, or else they come up at the bottom of search. When they strip out the HTML code, especially listing headers, they immediately rank higher in search.

My suggestion to you is if your sales are consistently coming in lower than you expect, or if when you search for your listings you can't find them, you need to rethink your listing strategy.

If you have a large number of listings on eBay begin by reworking fifty or one hundred of them. Strip the listing header out of some of your listings. Strip all of the HTML code out of another group. Give it a couple of days, and then verify what it does for your listing visibility and sales. This way you can see how your eBay listings are impacted by having HTML code in them.

HTML code in your listings has also been found to negatively impact your visibility in mobile search.

Why is this important?

Right now mobile purchases account for nearly one-half of all ecommerce sales. Over the next several years this number is expected to move closer to sixty percent. If your listings aren't showing up in mobile search you could be losing over fifty percent of your potential sales.

I tested listing visibility by searching for and displaying over fifty of my eBay listings using my iPhone. Ten of the listings didn't come up at all when I searched for them; the remainder of them displayed so-so on my iPhone.

The biggest problem I encountered occurred when I tried to view listings that included embedded pictures. The listings pulled up okay, and I could scroll through them fine, but I couldn't enlarge the pictures. Compare that to listings that use eBay's picture hosting service. Pictures that use eBay's photo service – display full screen on a phone or tablet. If there is more than one picture you can scroll through all of them by toggling the arrow that displays on the pictures. Embedded pictures remain their same wimpy size. Try it yourself, and decide which one you think will sell the most product for you.

My suggestion is to take a close look at your listings, and ensure they are optimized for mobile.

I think sellers concentrate too much on trying to make their listings look awesome, and not enough on the experience buyers receive. I know when I first started selling on eBay having a fancy listing template was at the top of my A-List. I invested thousands of dollars developing and tweaking it. In today's eBay marketplace you need to reevaluate this strategy. Test, test, and test again to determine which listing methods maximize your sales.

I love a good template and a fancy store, but they don't pay the bill if the sales don't follow.

Product Sourcing

I neglected product sourcing in the first edition of this book.

Where I did talk about it was when I explained to sellers how easy it is to find items you can sell around the house. My thought was new sellers should take baby steps, and get started by selling things they already have. I still think that's a good strategy to begin with. There's no sense jumping head-over-heels into something before you know if it's going to work for you or not.

Once you have ten or twenty sales under your belt you can start to think about what comes next.

When I first started selling online, Yahoo and eBay were the two big online auction players. I bought baseball card "lots" on Yahoo and resold them on eBay. A few years later when Yahoo shut down their auction site I started buying most of my inventory on eBay and reselling it there too. It's an awesome strategy, and it still works for me today. I rarely have to look anywhere else for new inventory.

The reason it works so well is most people don't see the real value in what they have.

I sell old magazine articles and prints. Most of my inventory comes from bound volumes sellers post on eBay for $5.00 to $25.00 each. When I buy a bound volume, I can break it down into anywhere from twenty to fifty articles and prints that I can easily resell for anywhere from $15.00 to $50.00 each. That makes for a really nice profit.

Of course, there are other costs associated with the items I sell. I have to buy holders for each separate article. I need to pay thousands of individual listing fees of five cents—each and every month. The result is my inventory is incredibly cheap, but my eBay fees can easily eat up a third or more of my profits.

It's a give and take situation I've found works well for the items I sell. For another seller, it may be a cluster F%#k. It just depends upon the items you sell, and your profit margins.

Another strategy that works for me is to keep an eye on eBay for poorly listed items. A lot of sellers don't put any thought into their listings. I've seen sellers list the first and second issues of *Sports Illustrated Magazine* from 1954 and 1955 without mentioning the baseball card inserts or showing pictures of them. When I spot these auctions I normally send a quick email to the seller to verify the cards are present and intact. If they are I pounce on the item.

You can find similar situations whether you sell clothes, books, sports cards, or whatever it is that interests you. My suggestion is to spend an hour every week scouring listings for similar opportunities. It's a good cheap source of inventory, and you never know what you're going to find.

Another good place to find inventory is your local Walmart, Target, TJ Maxx, or just about any retailer. Retail stores manage their inventory on a close time line. They receive seasonal items, sell them at full price for the first few weeks, and by the time they are midway through the season they start marking prices down. As they inch closer to the end of the season retailers are anxious to remove any leftover inventory so they dramatically slash prices – sometimes by 75 percent or more.

Smart sellers keep an eye out for these opportunities, and buy everything they can get their hands on. Some sellers shoot them back up on eBay right away. Profit minded sellers sock seasonal items away, and hold onto them until the start of the season next year. When they do this they can sell last year's closeouts at full price.

If you can scrape up a few extra bucks, or if you have some extra room on your credit cards, give this method of sourcing inventory a shot. Again, don't bet the bank trying to make one big score. Baby step it the first time or two to make sure the system will work for you.

If you buy your groceries at Walmart every week, spend a few minutes in the clearance aisles. Write down a few notes about what you find, and check what they're selling for on eBay when you get home. Or if you're really eager to get started you can check the going price on your cell phone while you're still in the clearance aisle.

For sellers who use this method a lot I'd recommend *Barcode Booty: How I found and sold $2 million of 'junk' on eBay and Amazon, And you can, too, using your phone* by Steve Weber. It will open up a whole new world of sourcing and selling opportunities for you.

Thrift stores like the Salvation Army, Good Will, and the DAV Store are another great source of inventory. These stores receive new inventory daily. You never know what's going to turn up there. Clothing sellers make a killing shopping at these stores, because they can find a good selection of brand name, gently used, and new clothes. Thrift stores are also a good source for books, DVD's, jewelry, and collectibles. Regular shoppers at thrift stores keep track of which days they change prices, run special promos, and keep an eye out for coupons that can save them an additional fifty percent on many of their purchases.

If you source a lot of your inventory at thrift stores, yard sales, and resale shops, I would recommend the book *9 Easy Ways to Start Making Money on eBay in 72 Hours or Less* by Michelle Angell. It's an excellent primer for new eBay sellers.

Yard sales, estate sales, and local auctions are another smart way to acquire inventory. Similar to shopping at thrift stores, you never know what you're going to find. My suggestion is to make some small purchases first to test the waters. Use your cell phone to research items before making bigger purchases. Some sellers have one person work the sale, and another at home by the computer to check prices as they call or text them.

Other sellers list items for neighbors, friends, and relatives. They take a cut of the selling price after fees, and pick up additional customers through referrals.

You can choose one of these methods, or a combination of them. The main thing is to find a system that works for you.

Be a Seller First

If I could give potential eBay sellers any advice, it would be to start out slow.

Take the time to really get a feel for eBay.

To be a good seller, you need to buy a few items first. You need to know what it's like to search eBay, trying to find the item you're looking for. You need to feel the thrill of winning a closely followed auction. You need to feel the disappointment of being outbid in the last few seconds of an auction you were winning all along.

There's a certain amount of anticipation that builds up waiting for your new book or game or pair of jeans to arrive in the mail.

Be sure to check out the packaging when your item is delivered.

What kind of appearance does the box or mailer make? Does it live up to your expectations? Hopefully it's not smashed, or the corners aren't dinged? Mailmen can be rough on your item.

If you haven't experienced the thrill of winning an auction, or the excitement of unpacking your new treasure, you're going to have trouble selling on eBay.

To be an eBay seller, you need to be an eBay buyer first.

Getting started

eBay Account. The first thing you're going to need is an eBay account.

The good news is – They're free, and you can sign up for one in less than five minutes. If you don't already have an eBay account, you can sign up for one now by visiting the sign in or register link. *https://signin.ebay.com/ws/eBayISAPI.dll?SignIn*

When you sign up you're going to be asked for some basic information. eBay will ask for your name and email address. Next you will be asked to supply a user name. This is how people will come to know you on eBay, so make sure you put some thought into it. If you know what you want to sell, it will make it easier.

I sell historical paper and ephemera, so my eBay moniker is history-bytes. It's short, simple, and says something about what I sell.

If you sell trains and your name is Dan, you could try danstrains.

If your name is Mona, and your reason for selling on eBay is to get some cash for Christmas presents, you could try: monaschristmascash.

If you can't come up with a good idea right now, don't sweat it. eBay lets you change your id every 30 days.

PayPal account. PayPal is the simplest and most popular payment method on eBay. If you don't have a PayPal account, you can get

one by visiting sign up for PayPal.
https://www.paypal.com/uk/webapps/mpp/account-selection

When you sign up you will be asked if you want a personal account or a business account. The choice is entirely up to you. If you go with the personal account, and later decide eBay selling is really your thing, you can upgrade to a business account then.

The great thing about PayPal is, as soon as your customer pays them, PayPal pays you. I would recommend that you sign up for a PayPal debit card as soon as possible. A PayPal debit card gives you immediate access to your money. If you transfer money to your bank account, it can take 3 to 5 days for the transfer to complete.

eBay also allows sellers to accept payment with a merchant credit card account, or it gives you the option to let the seller pay upon pick up.

Make it easy on yourself, and just accept payments through PayPal. It's the way 99 percent of your sellers are going to pay. Don't waste your time chasing other payment methods. It will just frustrate you.

Depending upon the type of items you sell, you're going to need a digital camera or scanner. Your cell phone camera will work just fine when you first start selling on eBay. Over time you will want to invest in a better camera because on eBay pictures are as good as money in the bank.

In these days of close-up photography, it's tough to visualize how big something is. You can say how big an item is. But if you really want potential buyers to get it, place a ruler by the item. A ruler with large numbers makes it easy for buyers to visualize the dimensions of the item they are buying. You can say six inches, but a picture will say it better—seeing is believing.

I've seen other sellers do this with a hundred-dollar bill. Everyone is familiar with money. Set your item down by a hundred-dollar bill, and people instantly make the connection about its size.

Finally, before you get started find a nice quiet spot where you can work without interruptions.

What Should You Sell?

If you're a new seller one of the toughest things about selling on eBay is figuring out what to sell.

It doesn't have to be that hard.

Most people get started on eBay by selling items they already have around the house. Look around you. You probably have a lot of great things you no longer use.

Do you have a pair of shoes you don't wear anymore? Have you upgraded your old cell phone in the past year? If you have kids did they outgrow any of their clothes? Remember that ugly sweater mom gave you for Christmas last year? Has anyone taken any college classes recently? Someone is going to need those textbooks.

We bought everyone Kindle Fire's last year after Christmas, but one of the kids decided she had to have an iPad instead. Now that Kindle spends most of its time locked away in a drawer—unused. I bet it could fetch a couple of bucks on eBay?

Do you get the idea? Everybody has items they no longer use. They're still great items. And, the chances are pretty good, there's somebody out there who'd be willing to pay you a few bucks to get them.

The reason most people don't get past this first step is because they have a hard time placing a value on the things around them. Sure you no longer use a land line phone, but chances are someone else will. You can drop the phone in the trash can, take it to Good Will – or you can take a long hard look at it, and see that phone for what it is - twenty-five bucks in your back pocket

Have you ever noticed, when you assign a dollar value to something, it appears more attractive?

Let's take another walk around the house, but this time, put on your "money vision" goggles.

What items did you miss the first time around?

Take a close look at your stamp collection. Do you collect baseball cards, Hummel figurines, or beer cans? Do you have any duplicates? Are there any items that no longer fit in with your collection? Often times, collections evolve over time, and you find yourself with a number of pieces that no longer really fit in with your current interests. People often upgrade their stamps and baseball cards over time as they find better copies. You start off with a filler card. When you can afford it, you swap it out for a better card. The good news is – you're not the only one who does this. Lots of other collectors do the same thing. That bumpy edged, creased Hank Aaron card may be just what another collector is looking for to complete a 1955 Topps set.

Does anyone in your house play video games? Most families today have three or four video games systems, many of which are no longer used. Take a few minutes to look for games the kids haven't played in a while. Chances are someone on eBay is looking for those games, or game systems.

My dad stashed all of our old toys, comic books, and such in the rafters of the garage. If I remember correctly we had Match Box cars, baseball cards, G I Joes, Rock Em Sock Em Robots, and lots of other cool stuff. Might be worth a trip to visit the parents, don't you think?

A quick glance at eBay shows Rock Em Sock Em Robots in good condition (with the original box) selling for $187.25, with 13 bids, and 14 hours to go. Somebody's going to have a nice payday!

Now I know there are going to be a few sour pusses out there who say they "got nothing." Like Charlie Brown at Halloween, all they've got is a bag full of rocks.

Suppose there really is nothing in your house you can sell. How are you going to earn some extra money?

Many times, it can be as easy as going to the store. Several Christmases ago my wife was shopping at Jo Ann Fabrics, and came across Bedazzler's discounted to five bucks. She had been watching them on eBay, and knew they were selling for $80 to $100 each. The first thing she did when she got home was check eBay. They were still selling for $80 to $100. She compared her Bedazzler to those selling on eBay, and sure enough – they were the same. Those eBay sellers didn't have any "magical Bedazzler's." They were just selling them for a whole lot more money than the ones she had just bought.

To make a long story short, we bought every Bedazzler Jo Ann Fabric's had, as well as all of the ones available from every JoAnn's store within fifty miles of us.

I sold 87 Bedazzler's for $50 to $75 over a six-week period. I probably could have gotten more money for them, but I unloaded them too quickly and flooded the market. (That's a lesson for another book.)

I like old books.

Occasionally I visit used bookstores when I'm searching for new items to sell. Last summer I ran across three county history books from the late 1800's. I purchased them for $100 to $125 each. Within two weeks, I sold them all on eBay for $250 to $400 each.

If you go to estate sales, they have boat loads of great stuff waiting for you to discover. Local auctions offer similar opportunities. Remember to put your "money vision" goggles on when you visit these places. You will be amazed by all of the profitable things you've been walking by for your entire life.

As you see, it doesn't take a lot of time, or effort to find items to sell. You just need to adjust the way you look at the things around you. You'll find yourself discovering profitable items everywhere you turn once you open your eyes to them.

Now that you have a better idea of the types of things you can sell, the next section of this book is going to cover the nitty-gritty of how to sell them. This is important to you because eBay has millions of sellers, and they're all competing with you to get the buyer's attention.

Luckily for you, most sellers have no idea what they have, or how to sell it.

eBay Selling 101

Let me repeat what I said in the last chapter.

Most sellers have no idea what they have, or how to sell it …

What's the secret to selling your items for the most money possible?

It's easy…

Put yourself in your buyer's shoes.

Take a moment to understand why a buyer would want the item you're selling. Ask yourself who is the ideal customer for it? Why would anyone want your old Kindle? What can they do with it? What could they do with it? Most people never think of it as anything other than a reading device. Did you?

My suggestion is to think about all of the ways an item can be used. Focus on several of these when you're crafting your pitch to buyers.

In the case of a Kindle, obviously you can use it to read e-books. Most sellers are going to leave it at that. It's easy. They don't have to put a whole lot of thought into it. Shoot a picture. Say I've got a Kindle Fire. Give me a hundred bucks.

Unfortunately, if you do the same thing as everyone else, your poor Kindle Fire is going to be lost in the crowd. A quick search shows 1208 of them on sale today.

If you really want to sell your item, you've got to put a little pizazz into your description. What if we said our Kindle is a great internet tablet for people on the go? Now that I think about it, my youngest daughter is always downloading movies and TV shows to watch on it. It's great for email, and oh yeah! With a USB cord, you can move your documents over to your Kindle to read and edit. And, did I mention, you can download music to your Kindle, and listen to it with your ear-buds.

It doesn't really matter what you're selling. You need to think outside of the box when you're listing items for sale on eBay.

I specialize in selling old books and magazines. Every day old volumes of *Harper's Magazine* from the 1850's to the early 1900's come up for sale on eBay. They consistently sell for $10 to $15 each. Most sellers post a picture of the dilapidated old leather cover falling apart from age, and say it's an old book in poor condition. Very few sellers open the book and look at all the great woodcut illustrations. Why not show a few of these? Perhaps it would help to list some of the contents? Or, provide a list of some of the articles readers can find inside? And, what would happen If you included a few interesting quotes from those articles? It's gonna take some extra time, but the odds are any time you spend enhancing your listing will mean the difference between selling your book for $10 or for $50.

Let me give you an example.

I've been following one particular book seller on eBay for five or six years now. He sells the same books as everyone else. The only difference is he receives dozens of bids on his books, and often sells them for $100 to $200, while his competitors who don't put as much work into their listings regularly receive $15 to $25 for the same books.

Any guesses why this seller receives so much more money for his books? He puts in the extra time and effort to craft a great description. He tells people what the book is about. He shares passages from it. And, he isn't stingy with pictures. The majority of his listings have twenty, or more pictures in them. Sure, you can say a book has great illustrations. A few well-chosen pictures will show buyers how great those illustrations are.

With all of that said, what's the perfect description?

What I suggest is you write the best description you can for each item. Don't worry about how long it takes. Concentrate on telling potential buyers everything they need to know to make an informed decision.

Let's Start Selling

The first thing you need to know is, selling on eBay isn't free. It's going to cost you a little money. The nice thing about eBay is sellers don't have to pay any fees up front. Normally eBay bills you about thirty days after you complete the sale. This gives you plenty of time to sell your item, and collect your payment, before you pay eBay.

As an eBay member without an eBay Store, eBay gives you an extra bonus for selling.

Your first fifty listings are FREE. You only pay final value fees if your item sells. If you run over fifty auctions in a month, the cost is 30 cents per listing. If you run an auction listing, and it sells, eBay will credit back your listing fees.

Used properly, and combined with your great items, this should give you more than enough opportunities to make some extra cash.

About eBay fees. Depending upon what you are selling, eBay is going to charge you 6% to 10% in final value fees when your item sells. It's a cost of doing business. Consider it your rent. If you have a store, you have to pay the landlord. If you list your stuff in the newspaper you have to pay for the ad. If you sell at a flea market you have to pay for your booth. eBay is no different. You have to pay to play.

eBay is the place where everybody gathers to checkout, and buy, other people's junk. If you're not selling on eBay, you're not going to make the extra money you want, need, and deserve.

Different Ways to Sell

If you're not familiar with eBay, there are several different ways to list your items for sale. The three main types of listings are:

1) Auction

2) Fixed Price

3) Classified Listings

Of the three, auction and fixed price listings are what you will be using most.

Auction listings allow potential buyers to bid against each other for your item, much as they would when they attend a local auction. The way it works is – bidders place what is called a "proxy bid." When they do this they tell eBay they are willing to spend up to a certain amount, $10.00, $15.00, whatever they set as their upper bid limit. From here eBay places your bid for you up to your maximum bid. If the seller starts her auction at $9.99, and your "proxy bid" is $25.00, eBay will place your bid for $9.99, the seller's minimum acceptable bid. If someone else places a bid, they will advance yours, up to your $25.00 limit.

Fixed price listings are similar to walking into your local Wal-Mart or Best Buy. You see a price on the shelf, and that's the price you pay. There's no bargaining, finagling, or whatever. The first person who agrees to pay the asking price gets the item.

Classified Listings are more informational. Businesses use them to get information out there about what they're doing. An example would be someone selling eBay training seminars. They can give information about their training seminars, and give you an email address or phone number to follow up with for more information (something not allowed in auction or fixed price listings).

eBay offers variations on the above listings everyone should consider using. The most important of these tools is **Buy-It-Now**. By adding buy-it-now to your auction listing you have the ability to start your item at a low price, yet reach for the sky. If someone exercises the buy-it-now option, the auction ends, and the bidder wins the item. If on the other hand, someone makes the minimum bid, the buy-it-now option disappears, and the only way to buy the item is by bidding on it.

The way I use buy-it-now is to set my starting price at the lowest price I am willing to accept. Then I set my buy-it-now price at three or four times my starting price. It's the price I would ideally like to receive.

Best offer is another spin eBay offers for fixed price auctions. Best offer works just the way it sounds. You price the item, and potential buyers can buy your item at the fixed price, or they can send you an offer. Be prepared to laugh a little, and cry a little, at some of the offers you are going to receive. I had one guy make a $1.00 offer on fifty different items I was selling at $25.00 each. You would think he'd have better things to do than waste both of our time making low ball offers.

What I've found is the majority of people will offer you between one-half and two-thirds of your asking price. Some buyers will low-ball you with a string of $5.00 offers; others are happy to save a few bucks to help them cover shipping costs.

The good news is eBay lets you totally automate this process.

When you set up the best offer option you can tell eBay to accept all offers over such and such a price, and to automatically decline all offers below a certain amount. This way you don't have to deal with any of those low-ball offers. The only offers eBay will send you are the ones that come in between the decline price, and the accept price. That way you can decide whether you want to accept the offer, or not.

For example, if I set the accept price at $17.00, and my decline price at $10.00, eBay will accept all offers I receive over $17.00. If an offer comes in under $10.00, they don't bother me with it. It someone makes an offer between $10.00 and $17.00, they send a message to the person making an offer to tell them the seller "is considering their offer." Then it's up to me. I can accept their offer. I can send a counter offer ("Hey - $10.00 is too low, but I would take $15.00"). Then we can bargain back and forth like this for another three tries.

Your First Listing

This section is going to cover everything you need to know to make your first sale on eBay. When you are done you will know how to write a compelling title that will bring hundreds of potential buyers to your listing, how to write a description that will leave potential buyers drooling for more, and how to shoot pictures that sell.

To get started selling click **sell** at the top of the eBay page, or visit the *Tell us what you want to sell page.*

If your item has a UPC or ISBN enter it when you are prompted. If it doesn't have either of these, or if you have a unique item, select browse categories. This will let you choose a category to list your item in. If you have an older book without an ISBN, select fiction or non-fiction, then drill down into the category that best describes your book. If you're selling a woman's leather jacket, select *women's clothing >> coats and jackets.*

Write a Compelling Title

eBay gives you 88 characters to describe your item. The more relevant keywords you pack into it the more people are going to see your item.

Why? Because different things are important to different people. Some people search for iPod; others search for iPod 8 GB; others are more interested in "certified;" still others for "Apple certified." If you want to buy on the cheap, but still get something good, you may want "refurbished."

Let's look at a few titles currently listed on eBay for the iPod Touch...

- Apple iPod Touch 4th Generation Black 8GB (Used)
- Apple iPod Touch 32 GB Black (4th Generation) Apple Certified Refurbished
- Great Condition!!! No reserve. Apple iPod Touch 4th Generation Black 32 GB
- Apple iPod Touch 4th Generation 8GB –MC55OLL- works great-camera-earphone
- Apple iPod Touch 4th Generation 16GB New in Factory Sealed Box

Now let's take a closer look at those titles. One thing that stands out about all of them is they are all loaded with keyword rich details.

- 8GB, 16 GB, 32 GB
- black / white
- 3rd generation / 4th generation
- Apple iPod Touch
- IPod touch
- factory sealed in box
- Apple Certified Refurbished
- Camera
- Earbuds

Yeah! It's an iPod, but that's only one small piece of the puzzle. Have you ever heard that old saying, the devil is in the details? What people really want is an iPod Touch with one, or all, of the above features. If you're title doesn't include the keywords a buyer is searching for, he is going to move on to the next listing.

When you write your title its sole purpose is to get potential buyers to stop, click into your auction, and take a closer look at your pictures and description.

Let's look at another item

If you type "Nike men's shoes" in the eBay search box, there are 219,158 pairs listed. That's like getting caught in rush hour traffic on the Eisenhower. Your shoes aren't going anywhere.

Without more details your poor shoes are going to be lost in the rush.

What we need to do is level the playing field. You have to think about what's important to people when they are shopping for a new pair of shoes.

Some of the things they're going to look for are:

- Size
- color
- style (athletic, loafer, dress, work boot)
- width (d, ee)
- model number
- new / used
- new in box
- easy returns
- men's / women's / children's

If you want to sell those shoes, you need to fit as many of these keywords as you can in the 88 characters eBay allows you for your title. If you miss just one, you're going to reduce your chances of making a sale.

A search for the following keywords (men's Nikes 10 ee new in box) reduced the number of pairs shown from 219,158 to six.

Obviously you have a better chance of selling those shoes when you're one of six pairs, rather than one of several hundred thousand.

Remember your title doesn't have to be a complete sentence. It doesn't even have to make sense when you read it. It just needs to have enough keywords in it, so potential buyers can easily find your item.

The takeaway here is to laser focus your title. If you're unsure which keywords should be in your title, search eBay to see which keywords other sellers are using in their listings. You can also search the manufacturers selling page for keyword ideas.

Picture it Sold

You've heard the old saying "a picture is worth a thousand words." On eBay, a picture can oftentimes be worth a thousand dollars.

You can have the best title, a great description, and a killer price, but if your pictures suck you're not going to sell anything.

When people are ready to buy something, especially expensive items, great pictures can really make the difference. The best example of this is your local car dealer. Car dealers don't stop with one picture. More often than not, you will find twenty to twenty-five pictures for every car they are selling. Car dealers understand, most customers shop on the internet before they come into the dealership to make a purchase.

As a result, car dealers give you a virtual tour of every car with the pictures they take. On the outside, they show you front, back, and both sides. They include at least one picture of the engine, a view into the trunk, the upper dash board, the odometer (showing the mileage), the floor – front and back, and close ups of any damage.

You can learn a lot about the type of pictures you need to include in your eBay listings by studying car dealer listings. The lighting is always perfect. Every picture is perfectly centered. Smart car dealers never use a bad picture. They know one bad picture can kill the entire deal.

Plan your pictures the same way.

Include at least one overall view of your item. Take close up detailed pictures of any designs. If there is damage – don't just say it in the description, shoot one or two pictures of the affected area. Let potential buyers decide for themselves how bad the damage is. That scratch you think defaces a 1955 Topps Willie Mays card, may not matter to a price conscious collector trying to finish his collection.

eBay lets you upload 12 free pictures with every listing. Include as many as you need to tell your story.

All photos are required to be a least 500 pixels along the largest edge. eBay suggests 1600 pixels for the best results. I size my pictures at 1000 pixels on the longest edge. Experiment with different picture sizes to decide what works best for you.

How do you resize your pictures?

If you only run a few auctions a month, MS Paint is the easiest, and least expensive way to resize your pictures. To do this, import your pictures into Paint, select the resize tool, and resave them. In my case, I normally scan 150 to 200 pictures a day. Resizing that many pictures manually would be a major time suck. I automate the process with Adobe Light Room. When I use Light Room, I can import all of my pictures with the click of a button, optimize them with two or three mouse clicks, and export them back to my desktop - all in less than five minutes.

The key takeaway here is to include as many pictures as you need to sell your item. If the lighting is off, or the picture is off center, retake it. A few extra minutes invested in redoing a poor picture will pay off when you make the sale.

Craft a Great Description

Think of your item description as your sales pitch. The more useful information you share about your item, the better your chances are of selling it at a premium price. Expand on all of those keywords you included in the title. Take your time to craft a compelling story that convinces potential buyers how much they need your item.

First, and foremost, be honest.

Mention any defects your item has. The last thing you want to do is make a sale, and have it blow up in your face, because of a scratch, or some other minor defect. The truth is most people aren't worried about minor flaws or defects. They just want to know about them before they make a purchase. What bothers people is finding out about problems after they've laid down their hard earned cash.

. . . . .

What makes a great item description?

You need to craft your listings to match how people read on the internet.

Most people are looking for something specific when they go to eBay. They want to know what you're selling, what it can do for them, what condition it's in, and how much it's going to cost them.

Make it easy for people to find the information they want, and you'll sell more stuff.

Use bold headlines. Include bullet points to highlight features or benefits. When you describe your item, use short paragraphs, composed of two or three sentences.

Work keywords from your title into your description. Salt them in your headlines, bullet points, and any other information you include.

Whatever you do, keep your description short. Don't include a bunch of unnecessary details or policies in your listing. Place them where they belong in the listing details.

Price Your Items to Sell

Congratulations. You've done it.

You've written a killer title loaded with keywords. Your description has left potential buyers drooling over your item. It tells a buyer everything they need to know to make an informed decision, and it appeals to their emotions

Now all you've got to do is price it right.

More sales are lost at this step, than anywhere else in the sales process. Too often, sellers become overly attached to their items. Especially, if it is an item they've owned since childhood, or one with a family history.

You see it happen on every episode of *Pawn Stars*. Rick, Cory, or Chum call in an expert to appraise an item. Their expert appraises the item at $1000, but the owner stubbornly clings to their belief that the item is worth more. Because the item is old, or has sentimental value, or they have so much money invested in it they feel a need to get a certain price, often times $500 or $1000 more than the expert appraised it at.

Bad idea! An item is only worth what someone is willing to pay for it.

Sometimes this works in your favor, other times you have to shrug your shoulders, and take what you can get.

In my case, I sell old magazine articles that have no set value. There's no official price, so I've learned to wing it. I play around with different price points until I find the one my items sell best at. I know from past experience what topics will sell for more money, or will sell quicker. If I have a hunch the item I'm selling may command a premium price, I jump my asking price twenty or thirty dollars. Many times I get it. If the item doesn't sell in a reasonable period of time I drop the price, and take what I can get for it.

Depending upon the items they sell, a lot of eBayer's don't have this luxury. Their items sell, day in and day out, in a very narrow price range. If you jump out of that price range – it's unlikely you're going to make a sale.

. . . . .

Here's one of the best ways to set your price to assure a quick sell through, especially if you are a new seller. Do a completed item search on eBay using the advanced search feature.

To do a completed item search, find the search box at the top of the eBay page. To the right of the word **SEARCH,** it will say **ADVANCED.** Click on **ADVANCED**, and it will take you to another set of search options.

Enter the keywords you want to search by. You can search in just one category, or search listings in all categories. A little further down the page where it says **search including,** be sure to check off by **completed listings**. As you scroll down the page there are a lot more options you can search by. Unless you are looking for some really specialized information, the only other two selections I would consider are: **Auction** and **Buy It Now**, under the **Selling Formats** category.

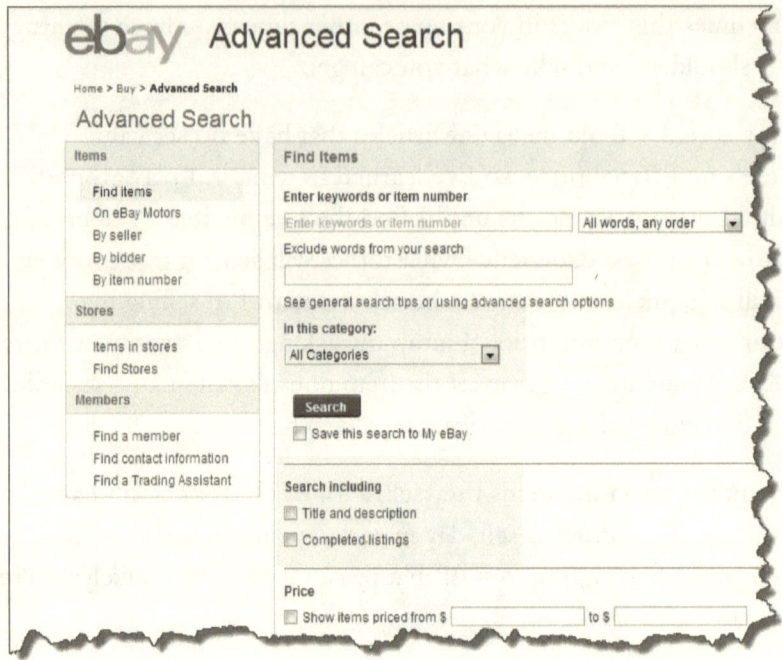

A quick check through completed listings for the last week or two will give you a good idea of the price range your item has recently sold in. You can drill down even deeper by clicking on the listings that sold for the most money or garnered the most bids.

Take a close look at the keywords the seller used in the title; what they said in the description; the type and number of pictures they included; and finally look at what price the seller started the listing at. No use reinventing the wheel, write all of this down, and include as much of it as you can in your own listings.

The biggest advantage of using completed item search is you can see exactly what items like yours have sold for. If enough items have sold you will have a very good idea how much money your item should sell for, and what price you should start the listing at.

There are several pricing theories you may want to consider.

One school of thought says you should price every item at 99 cents, and let the market set the price. This strategy works well with items that sell in large quantities, and normally sell within a tight price range. Electronics are a good example where this strategy can work for you. There are always plenty of buyers ready to pounce on an iPad, iPhone, or laptop. Starting your item at a penny, or 99 cents, is normally going to spark a bidding war that can bring you the best possible price.

Other people want to know their item is going to bring at least a minimum price. If you sell an item that normally goes for $100 to $125, price it at $85, and add a Buy-It-Now option for $125. This guarantees a minimum price if your item sells, and gives you a shot at getting a better price if someone exercises your Buy-It-Now.

Whatever you do, think really hard before you start collectibles or one of a kind items at 99 cents. Oftentimes a collectible, no matter how rare it is, will only draw one buyer at any given time. If you can't spark a bidding war that $100 or $500 item could easily end up selling for 99 cents.

Ship Like a Pro

There's no getting around it. Shipping is a pain in the ass. It's dirty. It's messy, and it takes forever.

The biggest thing to keep in mind about shipping is you are responsible for the item until the seller receives it. If it gets lost in the mail, you need to make good on it. If it arrives damaged, you need to make good on it. If your shipment arrives incomplete, and the buyer says all the pieces aren't there, you need to make good on it.

This tells you one thing.

Packaging is key. You need to pack your items properly. If you sell plates, glassware or other fragile items, you need to pack them so they can withstand being tossed around by a bunch of 800 pound gorillas. Don't laugh. Those packages are going to be bounced around on the back of the UPS truck, dropped on loading docks, and tossed around on sorting belts at the post office.

If you're mailing photos, or items that can be easily bent or folded, you need to package them in a sturdy mailer, and mark "Do not bend, or fold" all over the package. I don't know about your mail carrier, but my mail lady likes to bend and fold everything so she can cram it all in that tiny mail box.

The type of items you sell are going to affect how you ship your stuff, and what you should charge for shipping. Take a few moments before you list any item to think about how you're going to mail it. Will your item fit in a small box, or card stock mailer? Is it going to require lots of elaborate packing materials and sturdy corrugated boxes?

eBay allows you several ways to charge shipping fees. You can choose flat rate, where everyone pays the same shipping charge no matter where they live. With this method if you set your shipping fee at $5.00 everyone would pay $5.00, whether they live in the same state as you, or 2000 miles away in Alaska or Hawaii. You can also choose "calculated shipping." With calculated shipping you enter the weight of your item when you list it, and eBay automatically calculates shipping charges to any destination. By using calculated shipping, someone living closer to you normally pays less for shipping, making your item more attractive to them.

eBay gives you a choice of shipping methods. Among the choices you can offer are first class, media mail, priority mail, and express mail. When you offer choices buyers can elect a less expensive method of shipping, or chose a more expensive method that will get their item to them quicker.

Another obstacle you're going to bump up against is free shipping. eBay recommends free shipping. They suggest you absorb shipping and handling fees into your pricing. Before making any decision about shipping, I always look at what other sellers are doing with similar items. If everyone else is offering free shipping for similar items, you should probably join the pack. If the majority of sellers are charging for shipping, you should too.

. . . . .

eBay makes it easy for you to mail items.

You can print shipping labels directly from the item listing as soon as your buyer pays. To do this select **My eBay** at the top of the eBay page. Select **Sold** items in your selling manager. From here you can just go to the item you need to mail and click in the final column where it says sell similar. From the drop down menu select **print shipping labels**. From here you will be taken to the Print a shipping label page.

Fill in the weight and shipping method if they aren't already prepopulated for you. From there, it's a simple matter to select the shipping options you want—delivery confirmation, signature confirmation, and insurance.

Now I want to take a closer look at those last three option:

Delivery confirmation means the mailman scans your package when he leaves it at your customer's house. It is proof your item was delivered. If you print your mailing label through eBay or PayPal, delivery confirmation is included for free with most options. If you mail your item at the Post Office you need to fill out a special form, and pay the fee ($1.05 as of this writing).

Include delivery confirmation with every item you sell. It keeps you, and your buyer, honest. The first thing eBay and PayPal are going to do if the buyer starts an item not delivered case is check delivery confirmation. If it shows delivered – you win. If there's no delivery confirmation, you lose because there is no way to prove your item was ever shipped, let alone delivered.

Signature confirmation is similar to delivery confirmation, except the buyer has to sign for your package in order to receive it. eBay and PayPal require signature confirmation on orders valued at over $200. You can include it with the label you print on line (the fee is $2.90). Once again, if you do your shipping at the Post Office you need to fill out a separate form.

Insurance is an extra you can add to most packages. Insurance pays for damage, or loss of your items, while in transit. You don't have to purchase insurance. It is an option. What you do need to remember is: The seller is responsible for an item until it is delivered to the buyer in the condition you offered it for sale. If the item does not arrive, or arrives damaged, you are responsible.

Another thing to keep in mind is, eBay does not allow sellers to charge buyers for insurance. You can build it into your shipping cost, or into the price of your item. You cannot charge for it as a standalone option.

The take away here is to carefully pack and ship every item you sell. Select the shipping options, and extras, that are important to you. If you decide not to insure every package, pick a price point--fifty, or one hundred dollars, that you will buy insurance at, and stick to that. This way you can limit your losses in case something unfortunate happens.

Customer Service Is Everything

Selling on eBay is a lot like being a cast away on a tropical island. You're out there all by yourself, surrounded by an ocean of buyers, and the only way potential customers can tell you apart from other sellers is by looking at your feedback. If it's good, you're closer to being discovered, and making another sale. If it's bad, you're SOL.

Every time you sell an item the buyer has the opportunity to leave a feedback rating describing how well they thought you handled the transaction. They can leave a written comment about what they thought of your service and product. Buyers can also rate you in four categories including: item description, communication, how quickly you shipped their item, and cost of shipping.

It's called a five-star rating system because buyers can give you from one to five stars in each category.

You would think getting four stars out of five would be great. And it would in an ideal system, but in the eBay world, four out of five stars can get you thrown off the site for poor customer service. eBay considers 4.8 to 5.0 as excellent customer service. Anything below 4.6 is considered unsatisfactory, and you result in getting your selling privileges restricted.

That begs the question, how do you give outstanding customer service on eBay?

It all starts with your listing. You need to accurately describe the item you're selling. If it has any flaws you need to describe them completely. Add photographs where possible that highlight the problem areas.

Don't overcharge for shipping. Shipping is a big bugaboo on eBay right now. If customers even think you're overcharging for shipping, you risk getting negative feedback.

If you consistently receive poor feedback for shipping, the best thing to do may be to offer free shipping across the board. The reason for this is eBay automatically leaves you five-star feedback if you offer free shipping.

Respond quickly to customer emails. If someone asks questions before or after the sale respond immediately.

Answer all complaints quickly. Don't hope they will magically go away. Apologize profusely. Accept all blame for the problem, even if it's clear you're not at fault. When someone writes me to say they haven't received their item, even when they paid two days ago, and it's shipping to Japan, I start my email by saying:

"I'm sorry to hear you have not received your item yet. I did check my records. Your payment was received on ----, and it was mailed on ----. Normal delivery time is -----, so you should receive your item soon. Please keep me advised. Nick"

Notice – I didn't go off on my customer for expecting the impossible. I apologize. I explain the facts – when they paid, and when their item was mailed. Finally, I set expectations for delivery time, and I end by telling them it's okay to keep in touch.

Show concern. That's really all most people want.

What about requests for refunds?

My first year out of college I worked for Radio Shack. Every time someone requested a refund my manager would head for the back room as soon as the customer left, and start screaming and ranting. Quite a few times he smashed the returned item, bashing it against the wall, or crushing it on the floor. It didn't change the situation. It just made his employees really uncomfortable.

Here's the deal.

When you're selling online, and someone wants a refund, your reputation is at stake. The best thing you can do is apologize. eBay and PayPal are going to give the refund, regardless of your store policies. If you keep that thought in the back of your head, it makes sense to make yourself the hero, and take responsibility. Give the refund. Oftentimes you will find yourself pleasantly surprised. Many people don't want a refund. They just want to vent, or know someone was listening. I don't know how many times I offered a refund, and the customer settled down, and decided they really didn't want a refund. They could make do with the item—as is.

My Story

My story is typical of many eBay sellers.

I got my first taste of on line auctions in 1999. I had been following eBay and Yahoo Auctions for some time and one day I decided to take the plunge. I bought a couple baseball cards.

And then I bought some more, and some more. It was like an addiction.

Anyway, one thing led to another, and pretty soon I had this crazy idea that maybe I could sell some baseball cards, too. At this time, I was buying "lots" of 1954 and 1955 Topps baseball cards thinking I could piece together a set. Many of the cards were lower grade, with creases and bruised corners, but they were a start.

Whenever I got a better card it became part of my private collection. The other cards ended up in a cast off pile. As time went by I found myself with quite a few of these castoffs. And, they ended up being my first foray into auction selling.

My auctions were pretty unsophisticated at that time. Basically, I would scan a picture of the card, front and back, add a little description, and post it on eBay. I priced most of my cards between $1.00 and $5.00 based on how mangled they were.

But the thing is—people bought them. Sometimes I even had bidding wars erupt, where my cards would jump from $1.00 to $10.00, and even $20.00 occasionally. Pretty cool stuff.

This went on for probably six months, and I was doing ok. I wasn't really making any money, because even though I was selling several hundred dollars-worth of cards a month, I was buying just as much, or more. But it felt really good, because people were sending me money. Every day I received cash and checks in the mail, and dutifully I would package those baseball cards up, stuff them in an envelope, and mail them off to their new owners.

It was definitely fun. And to make it more interesting, back in those days, many people sent you cash, so many times, I had ten and twenty dollar bills falling out of all those envelopes.

Then one day I had one of those epiphany moments. I came across a listing for an old magazine article (not a whole magazine, just one article taken from a magazine). It made me stop. And think. What kind of a nutcase would buy, or sell, a magazine article?

I read his description. I looked at his pictures. He was asking $10.00.

I needed to know a little more. So I looked at other items he was selling. The guy had about fifteen or twenty of these magazine articles for sale. Some of them had bids. A couple of them had bids of $20.00, or more.

I checked his sold history. Over the past six months he had sold nearly one hundred magazine articles. Not bad for a few pieces of paper torn out of a musty old book.

I continued to sell my baseball cards. But over the next few weeks my thoughts kept returning to the guy selling magazine articles. I liked history. I liked books. It seemed like something I could do.

I decided to give it a whirl and purchased a copy of Harper's Magazine from 1865. It contained a good mix of articles. Some of them were about the Civil War, and others on historical places and events.

My investment was a whopping $15.00. And, like just about all of the items I sell, I bought it on eBay.

When my issue of Harper's arrived I paged through it. Before I took it apart, I made a list of which articles I was going to sell, how I was going to describe them, and how much I was going to ask for them.

Anyway, to make a long story short, I sold most of those articles pretty quickly. My $15.00 investment quickly turned into $250.00. And like my venture with baseball cards, I found myself buying more, and more, and still more, books to break apart and sell.

Today I have over 6,000 items listed on eBay, and just over 10,000 on Amazon.

Over the past thirteen years I have completed nearly 30,000 sales on eBay alone. I'm just ending my first year of selling on Amazon, and have racked up close to 200 sales there. It's proving to be a tough nut to crack compared to eBay, but I will make it happen.

After being laid off in 2004, I jumped into eBay full time. I went from making $500 a month to $5000 a month.

Before I started, I read every book I could get my hands on about how to sell on eBay. I contracted with a designer to create a custom listing template, and eBay store interface for me. I plugged my picture into every auction listing hoping to build trust into my listings. I offered a "100% Money Back Guarantee – No Questions Asked."

I jumped the number of listings in my eBay store from 500 to over 10,000. I was listing 400 items each and every week, and I was mailing out nearly 150 packages every week.

It was more work than having a job. I don't think there was a single week I clocked less than 70 hours. It was a seven-day work week.

This is true of every full time eBay seller I've ever talked with or read about. It's a 24 / 7 job.

You get hooked on it.

Many of my best sales came about by accident. Others happened because of deliberate planning, and a whole lot of luck.

In growing my business, I took a lot of chances.

I stretched the barrier every chance I could when it came to pricing my items. Many of the sellers in my category sold the same items I did for a whole lot less. I asked $25.00 or $30.00, they asked $5.00 or $10.00 for the same thing. I decided long ago to go for the gusto. My items have always sold better at a higher price.

I tried a lot of new things.

One of my great successes was selling newspapers. I bought every bound volume I could of the *Niles Weekly Register*. It was one of the first real National newspapers in America. Over time I was able to assemble almost a complete run from 1811 to 1833.

From 1812 to 1815 they contained great accounts of battles and leaders in the War of 1812. I read through every paper, and listed them on eBay one by one. I included excerpts of battlefield accounts in all of my listings. Two of them on the burning of the White House went for about $100 each. Another, from 1811, contained a printing of the Declaration of Independence, side-by-side with Jefferson's notes for it. That one garnered $250.

I even tried bundle a few of my items. Two of our presidents, Thomas Jefferson and John Adams, died on July 4, 1826. Four papers were dedicated to their lives, an account of their deaths, and news of their funerals. These papers sparked some of the hottest bidding any of my auctions ever received. The final price they sold for was over $500.

Another time I was bidding on an 1840's copy of George Catlin's *Letters and Notes*. I lost the bid. It sold for over $500. But another seller emailed me she had a copy she was willing to part with for $200. I jumped on it, and sold the individual pictures for over $3500. It was a nice score, and brought me lots of new customers.

I stumbled across eight bound volumes of the *Annals of Congress* from the 1830's for $10 each. They were filled with news of the battle at the Alamo and Mexican troop movements in Texas. The Mormon exodus from Illinois and Missouri was discussed over and over again, along with many other popular topics of the day. Once again, I was able to sell individual pages about the Alamo and the Mormon's for $100 or more – each.

If I could tell sellers anything about eBay, it would be to develop a niche no one else is selling in, and work it for all its worth.

Many of my customers have been with me since my first year on eBay. They know I'm always out there searching for new and unique historical collectibles. They appreciate that, and keep checking back to see what's next—what new articles I've discovered.

Over the years I've sold items to: The White House Historical Society, the Royal Museum in Jamaica, castles and historical societies all over the United States, Europe, Japan, China, Russia, Australia, and more. Hundreds of authors and publishers count on me for information when they are writing books, and illustrating magazine articles and books.

Museums buy illustrations and articles every day to augment their displays.

Probably the most off the wall sale I ever made was an article I found in a 1950's movie star magazine. There was a letter from a pregnant movie star to her unborn daughter. Fifty years later her daughter saw that article in one of my listings, and purchased a letter from her mom that she had never seen, or even knew existed.

In the thirteen years I've been selling on eBay technology has changed. People's wants and needs have changed. I now have my own website, digitalhistoryproject.com. I'm offering many of my more popular magazine articles as Kindle and Nook Books.

Who knows where your eBay journey will take you?

Thank you

Thanks again for reading my book. I really do care about your success, if you have any questions about this book, or about selling on eBay, you can always contact me by email at hi@nickvulich.com.

If you want to be successful selling on eBay, I would suggest you read every book you come across about selling on eBay—not just mine.

Every book, good or bad, will give you a few more ideas to add to your toolbox.

Bonus Excerpt

*(Here's an excerpt from one of my newest books, **eBay Bookkeeping Made Easy**. This section focuses on how to use GoDaddy Bookkeeping to track your sales, expenses, and profits. You can check the entire book out by following this link, eBay Bookkeeping Made Easy.)*

Getting started with GoDaddy Bookkeeping

GoDaddy Bookkeeping is available as an app you can download from eBay's applications bar. Amazon and Etsy sellers can check out the online version by visiting this link *http://www.godaddy.com/accounting/accounting-software.aspx?isc=gooob012&ci=87249.*

The service was originally known as Outright, and was taken over by GoDaddy last year. It's an online accounting solution that will serve the needs of most users. It automatically imports transaction data from your PayPal account, and posts it to the proper categories. Users can also synch their business credit cards and checking accounts with the service.

For sellers conducting business on multiple platforms GoDaddy Bookkeeping can import transaction data from eBay,

Amazon and Etsy. It also works with several invoicing services including FreshBooks, Shoeboxed, and Harvest.

Here's the least you need to know. GoDaddy Bookkeeping is available in the *Applications* tab on your *My eBay* page. Hover your mouse over *Applications* until it shows Manage Applications, click on this and scroll through the list of applications until you come to *Outright*. Click on *Outright*, and select *Try it Free*.

GoDaddy Bookkeeping is available as a monthly ($9.99) or yearly ($99.00) subscription. Choose your poison and follow the prompts to get started.

Overview

The first page you see is your account overview. It contains all of the basic information about your account. In the upper right corner, it shows your yearly profit or loss so you can tell at a glance where you stand. Below this is a graph that charts your income and expenses, a pie chart that shows your current month's expenses, and then a list of open invoices.

Below this is a section that shows Invoice Activity. Most online sellers aren't going to use this feature as all of your invoicing is done through eBay, Amazon, Etsy, and your ecommerce storefronts. If you're running a side business where your customers pay through PayPal this is where you would bill your customers for products or services sold.

In the left hand column, you'll see four small blue boxes. The first box is labeled *New This Week* and tracks your new sales, and any uncategorized expenses. To view your new transactions or uncategorized expenses click on the number, and it will take you to your general ledger.

The *Money I Have Box* lets you view the balances in your accounts – PayPal, Amazon, and any bank accounts you have connected.

The Money I Owe box shows your liabilities or the money you owe. Some of the accounts shown here are your eBay balance, and money owed to Amazon and Etsy for seller fees.

The last box is labeled *Taxes*. It shows you several key tax indicators for your business. The first line shows your estimated quarterly tax payment, and when it is due. The mileage line shows your year to date mileage expenses. When you click on mileage it takes you to your general ledger and lets you log your mileage. The last line shows your *Sales Tax Liability*, so you always know how much you owe.

Below the four blue boxes you should see two blue bars. *Add Account* lets you add your various seller accounts, PayPal Account, and any bank accounts you want to tie into GoDaddy Bookkeeping. *Refresh All* imports data from your connected accounts so that you're viewing the most recent information available.

If you scroll back up to the top of the page you'll see your six control tabs – Overview, Income, Expenses, Reports, Taxes, and Manage. When you click on any of these they open more program options.

Before I describe the control tabs there's one other item I should cover. Sometimes a tan bar will appear just below the control tab. It shows program alerts or problems GoDaddy Bookkeeping may be experiencing with your account. When you click on the Fix It highlight it will walk you through solving the problem so you can get your program up and running correctly again.

....

You can view your profit & loss statement anytime by clicking on the *view details* tab underneath where it says *(Year) Profit & Loss* on the GoDaddy Bookkeeping *Overview* page.

Your Profit & Loss statement gives you a quick overview of the financial health of your business. The top section shows your sources of income, and the bottom section details your expenses. The final line shows your "bottom line," or the actual profit or loss your business is making.

The default view for your P & L is the previous twelve months, but you have the option to change that any time you'd like. Scroll up to the top of the page under *Profit & Loss* where you see *ending*. You can choose the ending month or year, or you can change the time period to day, week, month, quarter, or year. To return to the chart select the chart icon on the right hand side.

If you want to take a closer look at a transaction all of the items on your P & L are clickable. Select the one you want to examine and it will take you to the general ledger page for that category.

Moving back down to the bottom of the page you will see two tabs at the far right side. Export lets you transfer P & L information to a Microsoft Excel file. Selecting print will give you a hard copy of your P & L.

Income

The income tab lets you manage your online income accounts. When you click on income it takes you to your general ledger page for income, and you can view your most recent transactions.

Once again, all of the transactions displayed are clickable. If you want to edit a transaction select it, and make the needed corrections.

What I recommend here is to set up categories for all of your income transactions so you can track where your money is coming from. When GoDaddy Bookkeeping imports income transactions it brings all of them in under the general "sales" heading. If you're just selling on one venue, such as eBay or Amazon, that's not a problem. If you sell across multiple platforms, it's important to know the source your money is coming from. This way you can take corrective action if a sales venue is underperforming.

The first thing you need to know is every time you make a sale GoDaddy Bookkeeping records it as two separate transactions. The merchandise portion is recorded under the "sales" heading. If postage was charged on the transaction it is recorded under the heading "shipping income."

If you want to add additional sales categories select a transaction, and then scroll down the page until you see a heading labeled *Good to Know*. Over to the right hand side you will see a link labeled *Manage Categories*. Select it. This shows you a chart of your current income categories. To add a category, select *New income Category*. Categorize it as *Business* or *Nonbusiness*, and then name the new category. After doing this you need to select a tax category. To tie the category you created to sales you would choose *gross receipts or sales*. Select *create*, and your new category is ready to use.

To give you an idea about how to use this, I added the following categories to my income account – eBay sales, Amazon, Bonanaza, *eBid*, bidStart, Kindle, Create Space, and Audible. By doing this I can keep separate tabs on each of my sales channels. It gives me better control over my business, and allows me to spot patterns early as they're beginning to emerge.

After you set up your income categories you need to assign each individual transaction to the proper category. The easiest way to do this is from the Overview page. Select *view details* to see your P & L. Click on *sales* in the income section of your P & L. This will pull up all of your unassigned items. Select each item separately, and assign it to the proper income account. This step is pretty straightforward and should take just a few moments a day.

Whenever you're working on your P & L you also want to take a look at your uncategorized expenses. They're listed at the bottom of the P & L, just before you see your bottom line. Most items are categorized when they're imported, but there are usually a few uncategorized items, either because you purchased from a new supplier and GoDaddy Bookkeeping doesn't know how to classify it, or because the items you purchased from that supplier may fit into several different expense categories. Click on the individual unclassified transactions and assign them to the proper category.

If you do this every time you open your program, it will only take a few minutes of your time, and it will ensure your P & L is up-to-date and accurate.

Expenses

When you select expenses it brings up the general ledger view for your business expenses.

Similar to the income category you can set up personalized categories to customize GoDaddy Bookkeeping for your business needs. Select an individual expense to enter the edit mode. Scroll down the page until you see the heading *Good to Know*. Move your mouse to the far right of the page and click on *manage categories*. Select *new expense category* and follow the prompts. Categorize the expense as a business or nonbusiness expense and name it. Scroll through the *tax category list* to tie your new expense to the proper category, and then select *Create*.

I would suggest setting up custom categories for your internet and cell phone providers, storage space rental, etc.

I find it useful to lump a few expense categories together. The main category I do this with is postage. I throw all of my shipping expenses in there – boxes, packing tape, stay free mailers, peanuts, you name it. The reason I do this is it makes it easier to compare my shipping expenses and shipping income. As long as the shipping income is equal to or more than my shipping expense, I know I'm on the right track. When they get out of whack it's time for an intervention to determine what went wrong.

With my other expenses my main concern is that they're consistent from month-to-month. If one month is way up without a similar bump in sales, it's time to investigate what happened. Sometime it's a special purchase I had the opportunity to make; sometimes a number was entered wrong. The key thing is to watch your numbers and react quickly when you see that something is out of whack.

Reports

When you select reports it brings you to your Profit and loss statement. GoDaddy bookkeeping always shows you the chart first. Select *view as table* to see your P & L Statement.

If you're running a business, you should know these numbers forwards and backwards. Growth is good, but I like to see consistent numbers across the board.

When I'm comparing my book sales numbers, the first thing I do is compare them with the last few months. If sales seem unusually low, I take a peek at last year's numbers to see if it's a seasonal trend. You should do the same thing.

Online sales are always slower in summer. They normally pick up by late August and run strong through spring. February is a little iffy – it can go either way. The first half of November can be the same way waiting for Christmas buying to kick in.

Key point: Use your P & L to help forecast fluctuations in your business. Study it for trends, where sales are increasing or decreasing, or where expenses are rising. Put on your detective hat and figure out what's happening. Doing this will make you a better business person, and help your business to grow stronger over the long haul.

Taxes

The taxes section helps you with three specific areas.

1) It provides your Schedule C information to make tax time a breeze. Just transfer over the numbers and you're ready to file. Keep in mind you're still going to need a tax advisor or a good tax program like TurboTax Business or HR Block Business. GoDaddy Bookkeeping doesn't figure the home office deduction, tax credits, etc. They just provide you with the raw numbers to fill out your Schedule C.

2) GoDaddy tracks your sales taxes due, so it's easy to file and submit your state reports. As long as you have eBay, Amazon, and Etsy set up to collect sales tax in your state, GoDaddy Bookkeeping will track all of the information for you.

3) Every time you log into your account you are able to see your estimated tax payments and the date they are due. This way the due date and the amount you owe won't sneak up on you.

Manage

When you select manage it displays a list of all the accounts you have connected to GoDaddy Bookkeeping. If any of the accounts have errors, you will see a tan bar displayed by them. Click on the blue *Fix It* link to take care of account issues.

If you want to connect more accounts, select *Add an Account* at the top of the page

....

Good to know

You can easily reassign categories if something appears is mis-categorized.

Most often when this happens it's because the program does not recognize how to classify the transaction. To fix the problem select the item that needs to be classified. At the far right it will say uncategorized item, select the correct category from the drop down box, and press save.

You will also need to re-categorize items when you make a non-business related purchase. GoDaddy Bookkeeping has a *personal expense* category you can assign the item to so it is removed from your business records. If you sell a personal item and receive payment for an item through your PayPal account, you can reassign it to the *personal income* category.

Best advice

Keep a close eye on your accounting program. Update it every few days. It's easier to catch errors when just a few items are displayed. If you let it go too long, a large list of items to re-categorize can seem overwhelming.

About the Author

My books offer short easy to read solutions to your ecommerce problems. Most of them can be read in under an hour. The information can be used to help you sell more products on eBay and Amazon, services on Fiverr, or eBooks on Amazon and Kindle.

Selling on line isn't a mystery. It doesn't even have to be difficult.

It's really all about getting started. Many people I've talked with have this crazy fear about putting things up for sale on eBay and Amazon. They think they have to do this and do that; they worry they don't know enough about what they're doing to do it right; they wonder what they should sell; and they worry about whether they can even do it or not.

That's where my books come in.

They take you hand-in-hand and walk you through getting started selling on eBay, Amazon, and Fiverr. They show you how to market your Kindle book.

My goal is to help you over the speed bumps, so you can be more successful from the get-go.

What are you waiting for?

Most of my books are available as audio books, so if you prefer to listen rather than read, be sure to check them out.

December 25th, 2015

Nick Vulich

Davenport, Iowa

Books by Nick Vulich

Don't like history? You're probably reading the wrong books.

Read this book, and you're gonna think, wow! Why didn't somebody tell me that? American history is full of strange paradoxes, and that's what makes it so interesting.

The truth is much of what we learn about history is a series of little white lies that over time have grown into tall tales.

* Why doesn't everyone know the Boston Massacre wasn't really a massacre? Subsequent testimony proved the soldiers fired in self-defense. The King Street riot was started by a group of four street thugs who got their rocks off attacking lone British soldiers. Sam Adams and Paul Revere twisted it into a massacre.

* And, if you think the Boston Tea Party was a response to British taxes that raised the price of tea in the colonies, think again. The Tea Act of 1773 actually reduced the price of tea paid by the colonists. The people hurt by the Tea Act were the smugglers. The lower price of tea undercut their business, and ensured that the East India Company would have a monopoly on tea.

* The South Carolina Nullification Congress of 1832 was a harbinger of things to come. The question was if a state disagrees with a federal law, does it have the right to nullify it, and disregard that law? Vice-president John C. Calhoun argued state's rights superseded federal laws. President Andrew Jackson believed to his dying day that Calhoun was a damned traitor, and that he should have strung him up from the nearest branch.

* The Black Hawk War was a mix-up of frontier madness, mayhem, and murder. Illinois Governor John Reynolds called out the militia and raised thousands of volunteer troops. General Winfield Scott marched his regulars half way across the country to Fort Armstrong at Rock Island. Lieutenant Colonel Zachary Taylor led a group of infantrymen in the fighting. In the end, it was a massacre that nearly wiped out the Sac tribe.

* In the fall of 1845 President Polk offered Mexico five million dollars if they would recognize the Southwestern Boundary of Texas at the Rio Grande. When Mexico refused his offer Polk decided to force the issue. He sent General Zachary Taylor and 3,000 troops to Corpus Christi, Texas. In March of 1846 General Taylor moved his forces into the disputed territory between the Rio Grande and Nueces Rivers. Soon after that, Mexico was provoked into a war with the United States.

* It has been said that James Buchanan was a "weak, timid, old man" who didn't do anything to prevent the Southern states from seceding. Some historians have even gone so far as to declare Buchanan was an "accessory after the fact." He was a president, Southern sympathizer, and traitor. But, was he?

* Imagine what it would be like to wake up, flip on the morning news, and discover Bradley Cooper or Ashton Kutcher assassinated President Obama. That's what happened in 1865. People were shocked when they learned John Wilkes Booth killed President Lincoln. Booth was one of the most popular actors of his day. He was young, just twenty-six years old, considered one of the most attractive men in America. At the time he killed Lincoln, Booth was pulling down $20,000 a year as an actor (that's roughly $300,000 in 2015 money). And, yet—he sacrificed it all for his political beliefs. What was going on in the mind of John Wilkes Booth?

I could tell you more, but you get the idea. Things aren't always what they appear to be. There are two sides to every story. All that stuff your teacher told you in school—it may, or may not be true.

Read this book, and decide for yourself which version you should believe.

Do you want to make more money selling on eBay?

1. Do you ever find yourself looking at successful sellers on eBay and thinking –They know something I don't.
2. They've probably got some kind of inside connection that lets them get products cheaper than I ever could.
3. They've already got the market sewed up, there's not any business left for me.

Have you ever told yourself –

1. If I had a little more money, I could buy the inventory I need to make a killing on eBay.
2. If I had a little more time, I'd be able to list enough items to be successful.
3. If I had a little more information, I could pick a killer product that would make me a million dollars selling on eBay.

Sounds crazy, doesn't it?

Every eBay book out there tells you the same thing. You need to find a great product that you can purchase at a reasonable price, and sell for a huge profit. If they don't tell you that, they tell you how easy it is to source product at garage sales, yard sales, flea markets, or the local thrift stores. And, my absolute favorite is the books that list 1001 things you can sell on eBay to make a huge profit. The only problem is half of the items they list are things you're unlikely to find – anywhere. Or, if you do a little research, you discover that fabulous selling price they told you was a one-time thing. The item is actually selling for much less now, if it is even selling at all.

Some books talk about drop shipping, or buying inventory wholesale from secret suppliers they use to make a killing selling on eBay and Amazon. Another eBay expert marketing his advice on Craigslist shows you how to source products on Amazon to sell on eBay. The secret is to discover fast selling items on Amazon, and list them for sale on eBay. When you make a sale on eBay – buy it on Amazon, and have the seller ship it to your customer. Of course, you need to purchase their entire system to make it work - $19.95 per month.

I've investigated all of these scams. And, yes – they are scams. If you buy from the majority of the "Special" wholesalers and drop shippers, you're going to discover most of the items they offer are selling on eBay for less than you paid "wholesale."

No matter what anyone tells you, selling on eBay isn't easy. It's not a sure thing. For every item that sells, another one or two items go unsold, or sell for far less than you hoped for.

eBay 2015 tells it like it is

I'm not going to tell you what to sell, where to buy it, or which items to buy. When someone guarantees you a profit they're normally feeding you a line of bull-hockey.

There's no hype, no BS, and no false promises. **eBay 2015** discusses the new eBay Seller Standards and how they affect you. It covers the problems eBay sellers encounter choosing which products to sell, how to keep accurate records, and how to ship items inexpensively and efficiently.

Learn how to –

1. Plan for success
2. Choose a niche
3. Ship like a pro
4. Sell international
5. Track your income and expenses

Selling on eBay isn't a game

You need to have a plan

eBay 2014 walks you through what it takes to sell on eBay. It answers all of your questions, and gives you ideas about how to get started and grow your eBay business.

Do you ever wonder how some sellers can grow a strong thriving business, while others barely scrape by?

Many times, I've watched two sellers as they are first starting out on eBay. Both sellers offer the exact same products and prices, yet one business skyrockets to the top of the charts selling thousands of items per month. The other business struggles to sell ten or fifteen items per month. They might even have the same basic look to their listings. On the face of it, it doesn't make sense.

Why does one eBay seller prosper, while another falls behind?

Is it a matter of luck? Does one eBay seller catch all of the breaks, while another is stuck holding doo doo? Believe it or not, many struggling sellers believe this. They think it's all a matter of luck. But, you and I know better. Don't we?

Sellers who succeed on eBay play by different rules

They don't leave anything to chance. They know that success requires a plan. You don't just move from Point A to Point B. You need to make it happen. And, that's what this book is all about. It gives you a strategy for selling on eBay.

You will learn

1. How to write titles that draw buyers into your listings and help them find what you are selling
2. How to take picture that show buyers what they need to know to say "This is the item I'm looking for!"
3. The anatomy of a great listing. What you should say. How you should say it. What not to say.
4. Why you need to stop guessing at prices for your items, and how to determine realistic prices that customers are willing to pay.
5. The smart way to ship your items so you can get your packages to your customers safely and on time.
6. How to rock customer service, and motivate your customers to leave five-star feed-back every time.

7. How to deal with eBay's constant string of updates and changes

Still not convinced?

Consider this.

- There are over 149 million active buyers on eBay.
- Last year they spent over $83 billion dollars on everything from paperclips to new cars and custom helicopters.
- Hundreds of thousands of small sellers are making $500, a $1000, even $2500 every month working part time from their kitchen table or garage.

How about you?

Are you making your fair share?

If not, this book will help you understand - selling on eBay isn't a game. You need to have a plan.

- **Get serious about your eBay selling**
- **Order this book - TODAY!**
- **Make more sales tomorrow - and everyday**

www.ingramcontent.com/pod-product-compliance
Lightning Source LLC
Chambersburg PA
CBHW020928180526
45163CB00007B/2934